Journey to Me

Journey to Me

A Meditation, A Confession, A Sermon, A Testimony, A Prayer

Phillis Cherie

ISBN-13: 978-1-7333659-0-1

First Edition
www.simplyphillischerie.com

Cover Photography by 'Sacred' Overstreet-Amos, Moon Reflections Photography

Acknowledgements

Every person on this journey has taught me something, in one way or another. There is not room enough to express my gratitude …
For my mom, Betty…I am grateful for the gift of my life that came through you. Thank you for opening up enough (over time) to tell me your story. It helps me understand my own.
My Guardian Angels - Anthony, Patrick, Brenda, Hillis….and more. My love for you outweighs the loss of you.
Billy - thanks for making a way for me – up, over, to , and through. You are a creative wonder. Consider this a Challenge!:)
Mark – "You and me like a tay ina wind" I love you Chicabee!
Alecia – My sho' nuff sister of my heart and soul…wherever I'm riding …I am glad I have you…reminding me to ride and live! You have my friendship, admiration, respect and love always.
Kevin - You have gingerly held this dream with me from the days of our first African-American studies and writing class 30 years ago all the way to this very day and every day (and rollercoaster) in-between. Thanks for knowing me and not judging me for any of it;).
Auntie's Divine Divas – Charita, Charisma, Bria, and Maya – may my butt-naked healing inform your own. Never forget your worth.
The Mims and Goodman Families – I love you for your strength, character, and humor instilled in me through the many tales told and untold.
My extended family – the Gillum and the Calhoun clan– thanks for the love, laughter, fellowship, and lessons. You are all crazy, and always my fam.

I am grateful for the layers of life-saving sisterhood the universe gifted to me: (They always knew I was up to something big)
The first (UNIC) : Eboni, Ayanna, Tanya, Denise, Jeanine, Sonja, Antricia
My amazing sorority sisters of Alpha Kappa Alpha Sorority, Incorporated®, *especially* my line sisters, W.D.O.A., – I love you amazing ladies with all my heart.
My Upper Room Crew (aka the disruptors) - Veronica, Jeri, and Vikki …what goes on in the room manifests in my life! I'm Alive!
My Wonder of Women (WOW)International sisters – the original 12 and the thousands to come who will "tell their stories, stand in their truth, and celebrate their wonder"….you have my sisterhood and support always.

Acknowledgements (cont.)

Finally,
When I think of home, I think of each of you: my heart, my courage, and my brain.
Winston, Ashlee, and Erin:
I am not perfect, I don't have all the answers.
Forgive me and love me through
And I will , with grace, promise to love and support each of you
as you find your own answers and your own way.

For all those whom I have loved, who have ever loved me, and who love me still...
may your travels be light...and may there always be love.

Foreword

By nature of our humanity and intrinsic to our very being is a natural desire to be seen, to be heard - validated, recognized, and appreciated. Loved.

When we engage our journey with heart, truth, and presence, we learn that life is graciously and generously offering another way: another way to give, another way to receive, another way to embrace and embody what we deeply and deservedly need. Sometimes the journey becomes an intentional sensually spiritual ride to a freedom we didn't realize we already owned.

You know that feeling you felt when the rollercoaster ride operator locked everyone in and suddenly you realized you couldn't get off? Just a few minutes before, you were happily standing in that long line with your friends waiting to get on. You were beaming with excitement as you stood in line looking at everyone screaming and laughing, enjoying the ride. Exhilaration filled your body while the colorful flashing lights filled your eyes. Now it's too late. It is your turn to ride and you can't get off.

We find ourselves moving like the roller coaster ride we did (or didn't) want to get on. Our need to feel the thrill superseded our fears and we got on anyway. Up and down, round and round, twisting and turning, screaming, yelling , and stomach-ulcer churning…suddenly we went way high up and dropped way deep down over and over, again and again, for what seemed like an eternity. Before we knew it, it was time to get off. As you stumble away, you find another long line of people waiting desperately to get on. But wait – you're still trying to feel your legs beneath you. Sound like life?

Journey to Me is a truth-telling affirmation and validation that you saw the caution lights, winding tracks, and risky heights. Although there was some fear, anticipation, and anxious feelings – you got on the ride and with a painstakingly beautiful boldness chose to reflect on it out loud. Not screaming and shouting to everyone but silently

Foreword (cont.)

and intimately healing and penning heartfelt confessions and meditations through lessons and sacred situations we all can relate to.

Before Phillis Cherie Mims-Gillum, M.D. became an accomplished physician to women, she was Phillis Cherie, a poet, a writer, a storyteller. Her voice was destined to be heard…at this time, in this way. Through **Journey to Me** you will not only find an invitation to speak your truth but a boldness to embrace it, love it, confront it, learn it, and share it.

What is the cat that's caught your tongue? "Spit it out!" What is the cancer eating you? Write a letter to your cancer. What dangerous ride have you been on? Get off! Run the other direction. Back to you. At your pace. When YOU are ready. This deadly asphyxiation trying to snuff out your voice cannot beat you! BREATHE.

Journey to Me confronts the false illusion that magically someone else has the prescription for our healing, the super fix for our freedom and our Cinderella slippers. We are challenged to resist the need for validation from those who want to make us ride that ride again and again – for a fee- as if you weren't already equipped with divine feminine medicinal powers to love and heal thyself.

Journey to Me is a journey to love. It is a thought provoking collection of poems and prayers that promises to inspire you to embrace every lesson love and life desires to teach. It compels you to understand and know that you can turn around, preach a sermon, and write your own freedom papers of validation and anticipation. As we journey authentically, we discover we are no superhuman, but a brilliant Supernova illuminating high and free for the world to experience and see.

Make **Journey to Me** your own. Don't rush through it, it won't let you. Read a piece, then set it down, meditate and come back again and again. Before you know it , **Journey to Me** will be your journey to you. It was for me.

Cheers to Phillis Cherie's **Journey to Me**!

Veronica Very
Founder and Visionary
Wonder of Women International

Intro

There is and will always be someone heading in the direction we are heading, en route to where we have already been, or coming from our (un)planned destination.

It's not just our labyrinth through which to work, our hill to climb, or our mountain to move – the journey belongs to us all.

With any luck we will wake up and stay awake for the important parts:

- Recognition of where we are
- Understanding where we have been and with whom
- Intentionally and deliberately defining where we are going.

Journey to Me is the ultimate example of the power of using your voice and telling your story in order to liberate and heal.
We all have a journey and we get to choose our own paths.
This collection is an urgent reminder that we must seize our right to define our paths instead of letting those paths define us.

Live like you mean it……and enjoy the journey!

Phillis Cherie

Table of Contents

Table of Contents **Page**

Table of Contents **Page**

***BONUS POEMS by Winston Alexander Gillum**

Welcome
to the
Journey

Journey to Me

My soul bleeds
Speckled with shards of glass
That I cannot see
As I scramble down here on the cutting room floor
Looking for my eyes
Or something I can recognize.
I don't know this girl,
Or this life
Photo-shopped
Into an instant'gram
Perfect for the book of faces.
Selective
Snaps and chats
Of a
fictitious biography
Validated by a thousand souls
Who could not care less
Applauding what they see
Even when they know…
Better.
The fallacy is deafening to me
Never knew how fragmented I was
Until I went to put myself back together.
Tried to flip through the timeline
to understand my story
Finding only a mismatch between what I see
And how I feel
Real memories say I am a goddess of the universe
Strong and unyielding
Yet here I am, reeling

Journey to Me (cont.)

Important landmarks missing from my life map
Smeared, erased, forgotten.

Trapped.

I scramble in fear
Trying to find the place that grounds me
The spot that establishes "You Are Here."

(Have I ceased to exist?)

It is accidental luck that
I find both the spot...and myself…
One fading,
The other flopping like a fish
Out of the sea
Yet drowning just the same.

Falling, not fixed,
Into a vortex, a black hole.

In death's valley… the lowest place I have ever been,
Life introduces me to myself
And I lean in and whisper to her
"If we stay here…we will die."
And so
The journey begins…….

My Story

I speak it
My story
And it falls forth from the corners of my mind
Where I've swept it.
Dredging up from the past
Layers of fear, doubt, worry, concern, hope, disappointments,
And dreams deferred.
I can hear it now.
See , taste , and feel the fear, doubt , worry , pain , concern, and wonder.
My story is a wonder.
It erupts from my soul,
Spills from my mouth like a juicy secret,
And lies wriggling on the ground in front of me gasping for air.
I'm encouraged as I wash the film of despair from my eyes
And when I open them
I can see
And my senses come alive
To reveal the wonder of me
Naked...and unashamed,
It is not as big as I thought it was,
This story that has ruled my life
And acted as a parasite of my soul
Numbed my life source
And written my obituary
Prematurely.

My Story (cont.)

It is actually smaller than me
Aesop's fable
A few hundred words
A few thousand tears
And lessons I have learned.
But still, smaller than me,
And clearly not enough to have done me in then
Because I am here now…WOW.
I breathe in fresh air
Into the spaces it once held
I breathe in hope, faith, love, and wisdom
And exhale my truth
Making it impossible for that story to return to the same spot
The same way
Ever again.
I am finally free.

Manuscripted

Fine sheets of alabaster paper
With ebon-hued ink
Carefully collated
An organized array of thoughts
Ideas and stories
A sequence of events
Arranged just so
    Orderly and sequential
A control freak's dream
Each element partitioned
Safe from the previous
Unmingled with the next
Labelled and ordered
Planned, implemented, and executed
Logically
I'm off on a journey
These pages ready, begging to be held together just so
    Bound with an artificial spine -
    All mine
    Protected with an airtight copyright
    First edition, only edition
    Shelved for future reference
    This is my life
    Perfectly manuscripted

        Enter……The Wind.

#Hashtag

#
The hashtag
used to be a pound sign,
before things got complicated
Placed to signal an end-
to enter or finish a thought
Not a trendy sign to begin an epiphany
It was simple before -
a pseudo-mystery
that always had me fooled
like peek-a-boo...and life.
Really, when I see it now
(and I see it everywhere)
it is the same as tic-tac–toe
Requiring neither wisdom nor skill
Just time
To reveal
That what comes before
Determines the after
Before

#Gullible #Blindhope #FingersCrossed
#iDidntKnow
#Hoodwinked
#KnewItAllAndNothingAtAll

After

#LivedALittle
#EyesWideOpen
#NoInnocenceNoPeace
#UntilYouKnowPeace
#TheEnd
And yet, the beginning#.

For My Youth

Age of Innocence

Some things I simply didn't know

At least then

I could still CHOOSE not to.

LoveYou

I didn't realize how long it had been
How hungry I am
Until you said it that way.
ILOVEYOU.
One word
Letters all pushed together
Period. Dot. The End.
Leaving no room for intrusion from words
That silently erode like But, If, Because.
You simply declared it.
Statement of fact, no reason needed.
Expecting no particular response.
Yet you were vulnerable enough, honest enough to tell me
That you hoped to one day hear me say the same.
Perhaps you hesitated for a millisecond
But it didn't stop you from saying it just so,
ILOVEYOU.
And it helped me nurture the kind of love
 I was created to give.
I tell you now
 ILOVEYOU!
Letters all pushed together
Period. Dot. The End.
So woulda, shoulda, coulda
Can't force their way in
Letting Can't , Don't, and Won't
Know
In no uncertain terms,
That they will never be welcome here.
Standing strong, but flexible
I will rest in this space
And LOVEYOU.

A Side of Love

Dreamed of love
With my eyes closed
And nose wide open
Before I knew
What a woman knows
Believed that we could be different than we are
Followed you
But couldn't see you were walking on your own
And there I was, a tag-a-long,
With my eyes closed

I woke up on the wrong side of love

No one sees me shield my heart from the blows
They say hang in there
And I can…..with my eyes closed
I am sitting on the wrong side of love.

You render me mute with your disdain
If I dare to utter anything that falls short of cosigning your brilliance
I doubt my own thoughts in the embers of your gas light
You remind me that I am not free
Yet you push me away
With your eyes closed.

I am here, on the other side of love.
You don't see me anymore.
You don't love me like before.
I woke up on the wrong side of love.
I see you now.
I don't breathe here anymore.
You wrestled my spirit to the floor
I woke up on the wrong side of love.
I don't breathe here anymore
I can't believe here anymore
You wrestled my spirit to the floor
And I woke up on the wrong side of love.

Mic Check

Testing, Testing, 1, 2, 3
Come in. Get on.

Sounds nice.
Is it safe?

Too much to do
To do you
I can't see right through you
To assess your molecules and your mystery
I don't know your truth
Or your history
And you don't know mine.

I like it bare
And I can tell you do too…
But reason whispers a word of caution
I need prophylactic protection
To avoid voluntary correction
Of a Misconception...
Or worse
A syndrome I can't run from.

Can you?

I RUN!

'Cause bullets bend corners
and I'm not feeling lucky
today.

Unbalanced

Stretched thin
Posted and planked
Across a pivot
Back and forth
High and Low
Completely out of your own control
You have become one with the game
Stagnant but for the
Kinetic energy powered by
Those who sit on the edge
Of your dignity and your sanity
Each pushing the limits
To see how far you'll go

Do you even remember
Which came first
The job…
Or the unbalanced life

See-Saw
Teeter –Totter
Work Hard
Play Harder
Tit for tat
This or that
You'll never get your life back
Until you stop the ride…
And get off.

Conversations with My Therapist #1:

Hell yeah I'm having homicidal and suicidal thoughts.
I could handle all this shit
If it happened
Sequentially
And not simultaneously.
See, it's too tumultuous.
Absolutely preposterous to expect a human
To stand
When all of this is happening
at once.
Like, can I press pause over here
So I can focus on this one thing?
Can I tap out
And tap back in?
Can I partition out my life
And deal with what I can deal
With
One thing at a time?
I'm not that weak
But I ain't strong enough
To bear the weight of a fusillade
Without bending
Especially when there is no promise of it ending
Unless I end somebody's life.

Note From My Therapist To My Employer

My client will not be filling out your " anonymous" engagement survey.
She has already entered into this arranged shotgun marriage
Because her qualifications
Meet your specifications
And as such she has committed to legally sanctioned servitude
She knows you will breed her to produce
Again and again
And when you've sucked the life out of her,
when she fails to be useful,
(Or before)
You will discard her.
She is utterly afraid to divorce you
And start over
or risk being alone
And so she stays.

I absolutely do not advise her
to consent to being engaged to you.
For engagement implies
something left to look forward to.
Engagement implies choice.
And the only choice she feels she has
Right now
Is whether to eat, die, or shoot up the place
Tread lightly…
your wife ain't happy.

Pieces

If I were mine to give
You'd have me –
Whole
But I have, in error,
Constructed an unholy partition
And all I have to give
Is pieces.
Do you dare wait for me
To deconstruct the walls
Around my passion, my purpose
And my pain
So I can stand
Undivided…
Or are you only patient enough
For the stuff that seeps through holes.
Beautiful specks
Created and discovered
Will scatter in the wind
And in the light
Mere fragments and floaters …
That's the trouble with pieces.

Ice Cubes

She was just starting to bud
When you preyed upon the glimpse of her possibility that you could control
and the vulnerability she tried to hide behind the strut
of a strong woman
able to hold her own.

You declared yourself the sun she needed, (all while throwing shade).
It was her good fate and fortune
that you let her in
luring her with the idea that she was lucky
resting solely on *others* professing what she had won.
A trap was set, the game begun
with her attempts to prove that she could love you.

You baited her with the reminder of everything she had yet to do...see...or become…
and you won.

Nullifying naysayers with a competitive exuberance
in synergy with proving them all wrong .
She was your lovely leprechaun
found at the end of an urban rainbow.
You siphoned her pot of gold
and then paused to show her how empty a treasure she had become.
Meeting "I love you"
with "ditto" or "same here"
year after year
until even they disappeared behind a guttural grunt.

You followed the laws of consumer mind-control…
limit supply, thereby creating demand-
and she scrambled in Black -Friday mentality for your love.

Ice Cubes (cont)

Things she thought she needed to survive,
you parceled them out in emotionless measured fits.
She turned tricks hoping to be seen
While you look bored long enough to cause her to doubt
the genuineness of her gifts.

Diabolically dismissive, the more she bloomed
so she was driven to explore her flowers in private,
to hide the ornateness of her being.

She showed up as less than a full bouquet so she could meet the capacity of your tiny vessel,
leaving more and more of herself behind.

A million parts that you would not hold -
her dreams, hopes and visions.
You were afraid they would burn your tongue and leave you hurting and alone
so you dropped ice cubes in her hot tea,
(ice cubes in her hot tea, ice cubes in her hot tea)
to water her down
until the contents were so faded and weak.
that she almost lost the taste for herself.

But instead, …
she ran
to get a new cup…..
(and perhaps a new fountain).

You're so dismissive
you think her gifts were only valid through you.
You're so dismissive
you won't read this to know it's about you, yes you.
You'll probably tear her down because it rings true
won't you?...won't you?

Sweet Serpent

He never questioned
my decision to stay

He just showed me
where I can come
anytime.

Haiku #1: Self-Discovery

Touched myself again

Parts of me feel so damn good

Someday you'll agree.

Knitted

This cardigan wears me.
It has done so for years.
Draping my frame,
it clings to the memories
of who I used to be
and the reality of who I have become.
Oh the stories those threads could tell
if they too weren't relegated to inanimate silence.

Tried to preserve my smock with a fancy lint shaver -
stuffed those little balls of lint somewhere
(in my voice box perhaps– muffling my truth?).

A luscious blend of cotton, acrylic, and wool
once, and still, a crisp and perfect fit,
for I, too, have become shapeless.
A little frayed at the ends,
fashionably so,
if being worn down and broken-in is ever fashionable
...for a human.

It wears me well
in my faded shell,
reflecting muted shades and hues
with reverence.

A barrier from the cold world
that warms and comforts in the icy frigidity
yet fine-spun fiberglass
that prickles in the heat,
so much so that I can't stand it
without scratching off my skin.

Knitted (cont.)

It's threadbare in spots,
sure soon to bear a hole
that rivals the holes that have started coalescing in me.
I pull it snug around my chin often
and inhale the scent of safety.
This cloak reminds me …of me,
before I started unraveling.

Unstoppable glass prisms and waterfalls appear
and I gasp, looking for the loose threads I found long ago.
The ones knotted and tucked in-between the seed stitch
threatening to untwist
and fall apart.
Distracted by the complexity of it all,
I grab the string and commit to
unraveling.
I feel smothered by a smock of my own design

And I am unable to stop
unhitching the needlework.
And then it seems, I stall at the seams.
Halted, as if it, and I, will yet resist and withstand.
But the pause is fleeting
and fibers fall
mocking me for the way I have weaved my life.

I stand, finally, in a pile of twisted Alpaca and Hemp
Worn...but finally free
from the shrug that has worn me
for years.

The Whole Me!

Came close to failure-
altered course to persevere
Recognized losing battles
And flat out quit
With some regret
And perpetual hope.
I never knew how it felt
To feel defeated
But this is it.

I'd rather give up half
To keep
The WHOLE of me.
The cost would be so great
That some would choose to stay
But I can't justify paying the price
Of that life.

Tell me what you feel you've earned, by tenure-
We both know it is not what you deserve

I reserve the right
To hold tight
To the pieces of my heart.

And when you are gone

I will put them back together

Relinquish the idea
Of unrestricted control of me.

I
Above All
Deserve to have The WHOLE of me.

Ch*/g!

I was cursing you
You were cursing me
And all I did was Ch*/g!
Or ask you to.
You fired back profane–ities
You won't give me the power
To Ch*/g! you.
We lie pulseless.
I was only trying to grow with you
Even dead things Ch*/g!
How dare I curse and disrespect you
I see you recoil…. Ch*/g! must be filthy dirty thing
And yet you let me F*ck you
Grab my head as I suck you
Give me all that D$ck
And talk about how good my Sh!t is…
And how you hope I'll never Ch*/g!

You had me so convinced that I was wrong
That I started cursing myself
And I was merciless
D#mn B^tch
Why'd you Ch*/g!
Ch*/g! back
F*ck, Sh!t, D#mn
Can you stop that…

Ch*/g!ng.

It's an unpredictable metamorphosis
I'm not who I was
….and you are
So I buried you this year
And I am here
Ch*/g!d.

Libido

I see you coming and forget that I know how to breathe
You call my name and the distance between us is just a memory
You move so smooth, …..unphased
But subtly you let me know
You… see… me
It feels so good to be seen.
Between my thighs I feel
The heat of iniquity creeping in
Behind these eyes I dream with longing
For the new adventure I hope we will begin.
As we must,
We part, and night envelopes day.
Embrace, hesitate, a kiss,
And we go our separate ways.

At home
I'm alone…and yet I'm not
I stand beneath hot shower mist
Caressing my skin,
Rising within
A newness that didn't exist before
I turn my head to my shoulder
And kiss.
It is wet …and warm.
Blissfully I imagine that it is you
Inhaling me.
I stick out my tongue to taste
As far as flexibility will allow
Palms down my side, small of my back
I close my eyes
And rest my breasts
Where I imagine your mouth to be

Libido (cont)

Uninhibited passion, without parameters
Quickens my pulse
As I ride the waves of my desire to heights not fully explored.
I feel the purring of orgasmic melodies rising in my throat
And part my lips allowing them to pierce the air .

Here, I come.
Floating high
Landing warm
Cresting and resting
From the erotic flight
That will get me through this night
Until the dawn.

I will rise
Still dreaming.

It's no surprise
That I spend night and day
longing for you…
But you make me
Want me,
And that is new.

Conversations with My Therapist #2:

The things that I remember have already fucked me.

I laugh, I cry, I tremble
I freeze...I run.

There is no way in hell I am trying to root up
The things that I forgot.

It probably isn't wise.

A favorite memory?
Sitting in the front of my father's cab
Reading to passengers from my children's bible
A gift from Sweetie Pie…

Makes
me
recall
That one time a passenger tried to rob my dad at gunpoint.
He came home with the gun.
(I was so afraid the cops would come).
But it stayed hidden
Until the time my brother locked it in a trunk with his comic books
Because my parents were fighting… again
And he was afraid something would happen
And the cops would *have* to come.

Do you see how memories run on?

Let's go to something sweeter,
What was my favorite treat?
A hot pizza from Italian Fiesta, a Maxwell Street polish
With grilled onions, mustard, and peppers
Or a dozen Dunkin' Donuts
(When they were actually good)

Conversations with My Therapist #2 (cont.)

Gifts of the Gods held in the hands of a giant
Who would ascend the stairs three at a time
To deliver them to my brothers and I

Instantly
reminds
me
of my grief
For the brothers who have gone
Cancers that eroded their bodies
While their minds and spirits yet thrived
Men Down!
Yet I am still alive.

What?!

You say it's time to go?

This is precisely why I don't want to go deeper with you.

You unroof my pain
And make me wait a week
to pay you
To do it again.
All the while you applaud me for my healing.

Cataracts

Love
Is
A
Big
Fat
Cataract!

Fall out of love
And See!

Haiku #2: Him

He sits next to me

Smells so good I am dizzy

I should just lick him.

Haiku #3: You

Now I notice him

Your bullshit was my LASIK

Wanted you to know

Forever, Until

Someday, somebody will be mad at me
For blocking their way to you.
I am rooted in that space in your heart
Transfixed in your brain
And I am staying
As long as I am allowed to.
We can make believe
That there is only this
Me……..and you
And the dreams that drown out fears.
A safe space to surrender
Passionately,
Passionate love is defeating,
And we have chosen to let each other win
Until we find ourselves again.

Take only as much as you can afford to give
And still survive.

Symbiotic Parasites of Pleasure
Together
Forever
Until.

Say That!

I wasn't ashamed of what I had done
I really didn't try hard to hide it
You had every right to call me on my bullshit
The only problem I had
With your come to Jesus meeting
Is that you thought you were Jesus.

Tell me how this works
You don't want to hold me
But you refuse to let me go

All along we've been playing a game of rise and fly
You act so alarmed that I am moving on.
Your UNO
preceded
my out.

I no longer like the woman you were in love with
So one of us had to die.
You should put some flowers on her grave.
And while you are at it
Decide if this new woman
Is one you would like to get to know
Can you stand to watch me grow?

You hesitated…
I'll see if the plot next to the old me is available…for you.

Cigar Talk

Part your lips.
Take me in.
Let me rest there
As you light the flame
And start the spark
That warms my insides.
As heat rises,
Inhale me.
Let me seep down your throat
On the path to your soul
So as not to choke.
I can be a lot.
Inhale slowly
And hold me in,
Don't blow me off.
Don't let go so quickly.
Let me flow between each fiber of your being,
Seep into your cells,
Nudge your neurons
So you know you are alive.
Let me awake in you
Then lull you
To the safe place
Where we are
Love is
And hope lives.
I'm flowing with you,
Through you.
I am you.
We are one.
This is love.

Blazing

This is the year of
Yes, I can…But NO…I WILL NOT !
I'm sick of burnout!
Let me set your expectations of me on fire
And watch them burn instead.
Stop the churning inside that says
That I should… just because I can,
or because you entice my competitive spirit
With accolades and titles
Or words that suggest
That if I don't, someone else will
And will receive all the credit.
Give it to them then
And the debit will be theirs too
I can no longer afford the debt that comes
With chasing another's goals and dreams as if they were my own.
When I put in earplugs
I can no longer hear, or sing,
the song of over-extension
That has meaning…at least to me.
So I am putting my finger in my ears,
Sticking out my tongue,
And patting my foot to my own tune-
Banging my own drum
Dancing to a tempo that doesn't leave me
Frazzled and Blue.
And you…my friend
Can just find someone else to do
What you were just about to suggest was divinely designed for me.
I'm Aflame…and THIS…s the year I OUTBURN you!

Team Player (urban definition)

Sometimes I work with smart people ….
Sometimes I don't.

Homeless people have nothing to lose
So they will say anything.
I won't.

I like my house.

Diversity Training for the Conscious-minded:

Me, Black, Woke, Evolved

I would beat the shit out of you, but I remember that slavery was the act of beating our people into submission and slavery in all forms was and is wrong. So let's talk it out and negotiate an alternative punishment that takes into account both your lack of understanding and your feelings.

Me, Black, Woke
I would beat the shit out of you , but I remember that slavery was the act of beating our people into submission and slavery in all forms was and is wrong.

Me, Black
I will beat the shit out of you
…..

Me
You feel lucky…try me.

Rope Drop

Tuck your dirty laundry away in neat little piles
Then run around showing your ENTIRE ass.
Not a cute look,
Mr. and Mrs. Petty …
Your slip is showing.

I will not play tug-of-war with the likes of you.

I learned long ago
Not to get in a pissing contest with old (or crazy) people
They will totally take off their diaper
And slap you in the face.

So with restraint, maturity, and grace
I will ignore the tantrums of hurt little boys and bitter girls
And two-step past the covert attempts to shame or hurt

I will simply shake my head
And write a book about it.

The proceeds will pay for my therapy.

The Scarlet Alphabet

They sling a scarlet letter her way
To maim, or perhaps to shame her
She picks it up, adding it to her collection

A scarlet alphabet
Frames her like a coat of many colors
And it fills them with more hate and rage
Than she has fear
See how it draws people near
Although they hoped it would push them all away.

She is more than their summation of her.
Not easily reduced to initializations
Or silenced by intimidation
They conspire to call her out and name her
Yet she reclaims herself with every letter
Free of charge she edits their insults…and makes them better
Or at least a clearer picture of who she is.

They will never see her beyond the walls of their own pain from which they cast their stones.

Haiku #4: The Book of Revelation

Sure, I know your kiss

Soft lips like this had Judas

Betrayal soon come

Snow White

Don't ask the mirror who's the fairest of them all
Unless you are pretty confident that your stuff is tight
And even then,
you may get your feelings hurt …
Forgive the world
And pray your way forward
Beyond any impurity of the past

But know this
You ain't done a thing
Until you've gazed into the mirror
Asked for forgiveness
And with words and deeds
said YES!

Homework from My Therapist:

Who was it that modeled friendships and relationships?
What did they say that was right?
What did they do that was wrong?
What did you learn through trials and errors of your own?

Unrealistic benchmarks of a perfection
That can never be met or achieved
They didn't tell you
That a quest to be the "be all"
Would be the "end all" of you

Love is reciprocity.
True love has infinite power
To levitate and elevate exponentially
And real power wastes no energy or oil
On the need to control,
It relinquishes the impulse
To micromanage …or manipulate
You don't have to explain a thing to real love.

Neither flower nor weed
Asks permission to grow or die
They both simply recognize what is available to them
……and what is not
And respond accordingly
They never warned that soil can turn hostile
And the once fertile ground where you planted yourself,
Could stunt your growth and poison your roots
They never said that sometimes you would need to be
(or choose to be) repotted.

They told you how to stand and thrive
In the shit provided by others
But forgot to school you on what to do
When you are knee-deep in a waste that is self-produced
Or how to admit an uncomfortable truth….

Homework from My Therapist (cont.)

They oozed it and you mastered it
Sensuality and sexuality that can make a person weak in the knees
They didn't say anything to you about how to show up unarmed
And meet another soul in the wounded and bruised corners of their heart
While showing them your own…they forgot that part

They said out loud –" You get to choose "
And then muttered and mumbled
"You're nothing until you're chosen"
They didn't warn that if all you seek is being chosen
You'll sit and collect dust upon a shelf
A hollow shell of who you were meant to be

They only said speak when spoken to,
And use your words wisely.
They neglected to mention the power and the duality of Silence
Deliberate and intentional speaking ...or the surrendering of a voice
And thereby a soul.

Silence
A solitary confinement
That either saves you or drives you insane
Time served with early parole for good behavior
Or a death sentence
Confining you to a cell that will hold the un-held you
Until you are set free on a green mile
That will lead to your execution.

They never said opening your heart to love
will kill you …and resurrect you
But they tried,
Again and again to get it right
Choosing love (signing up to both live and die)
Because there is truly nothing better.

Sick-Bed

A virus courses through my body
Permeates my brain
Seers my heart
A disease with no name
Except
YOU
Causing Pain.
I hear you speak
Words that sink in
To defy my reality -
I am sick.
You wipe the sweat from my feverish brow
With a cloth
Lingering too long over my nose…muzzling my mouth
And for a split second
I don't know what you will do.
There is turmoil within
And no rhythm to this heartbeat
with you.
I am a cyanotic blue
And my breath is shallow
Heart hallowed by this thing
And I don't feel well
I keep company with leeches
That bleed my soul
And leave me
Wholly spent
Dry heaving, still

Though I've nothing left to give
But I have the will
To Live
And I don't feel alive with you
…And then I do
It is fleeting, when the fever breaks
I hope that I am wrong
That what ails me is only transient

Sick-Bed (cont.)

A million-dollar workup
The results are in
And it is clear…as I feared
This silent killer
Is indolent......permanent
As long as you ARE -
And therein lies my truth
I don't feel well with you.
Perhaps the Panacea I seek
Will never be known

One day
I will gather wits
Summon strength
To unhook myself
From this unsupported existence
And go
In search of LIFE.
Perhaps the prognosis for me
Will simply be
To not feel well
But at least then
You won't have to stand on sick-watch
And I
I won't have to worry about you

Shh!

We're giving each other the silent treatment
Again
Hallelujah!!!

When we cut out all the small talk
I realize that you're all talk
And I don't have much to say.
And here I thought I had lost my voice.

I am not the one with pressured speech
Although I admit I do emit the static of white noise
And together
we can no longer hear
Or be heard.

Your words confuse the picture
A dance of smoke and mirrors
With selective secrets
And scripted truths.

AH-HA moments
Are more a game of Gotcha
And I have often wished that the cat
Would come and find your tongue.

I enjoy the silence now.

Are you speaking again…….so soon?

I won't shush you

But I let your words
Float away- untouched.

Asphyxiation

You might as well
take your soft hands
Place them around my bare neck
Set the fatty pads of your thumbs
Into the hollow indentation
And press …slowly
So I can feel each millimeter of compression
Smell my own fear rising
Until I whimper for you to stop
Until my voice box can withstand no more.
You might as well keep pressing
Until there is no air left to flow
Until you hear the crunch of cartilage
And witness my eyes
As they roll to the heavens
For the only place true mercy will be found
You might as well do it now
End it all
If the price for your civility is my silence.

Global Warming

There is no such thing as global warming.
Scientists keep producing facts
But I am convinced it's a myth-
It can't exist in your midst
Under you watchful eye
That glares with the stares of a million glaciers
The likes of which the world has never known
Before our now.
I see what you have done
Crystallized the tears,
The missteps, the fears
Of all these years
And shaped them like tiny icicles.
I feel the spears
Every time I dare to rise, to speak, or to be
If you do not approve

I've made them too.
There is love yet left in me
The ice I make is frigid … but less rigid

Touch and you will find
It melts with time
Although not with ease.
How long before you knock me to my knees
Again
Teaching me a lesson
I have tried not to learn.
There is no global warming.

There used to be…for you and I
Love flowed freely,
Rushing rapids
A calm lake

Global Warming (cont)

A brook bubbling over a rocky bed

'Til the rocks became a dam.

I stand as she did on the Titanic
Arms spread wide
At the bow
Glaring into the torrent
Declaring foolishly
That my boat is bigger
My tanks still fueled.
I see the storm
Try to seize the storm
Surely I can penetrate these cubes.

If there was global warming
It would get hotter
And you would melt when you see me coming to you.

I remember history
It wasn't just the tip
of the iceberg
but all that lay beneath…
I feel the frost biting the air
And I know something sinister lies there.
I am sinking fast
Will there be anyone to claim my wreckage
And turn this sordid story into a beautiful tune.

Could a shoulder be any colder than this?

If there were Global Warming
Then these warm tears
And this tiny ice pick I wield
Would be enough.

Phillis Cherie

Dream Cruise

She is ready to go for a spin.
Freshly washed and waxed…glistening.
Moisture pools, beads, and rolls
Waiting to be wiped away by a rhythmic wand
That will clear my view.
I'm pushing the button
To start the engine
And listening for the roar that says
I'm ready to roll.
I'm turning on my headlights
Aiming them
Shining bright as they point the way.
I am shifting gears to steer her
To the lucky passenger who's turn it is to ride deep inside
The front ...or the back
I haven't yet decided
But I am going to take them
Where I want to be
And hope they enjoy the ride
From idle to full throttle
In tight spaces
Sharp turns
Making donuts, round and round
Dipping down
Rising to taste the thrill of speed
On an open road
As I floor it to the limit
And take my hands off the wheel
Hydroplaning, in a tailspin, free-falling, floating , rolling to a stop.
I'm gonna listen for a while
Before I shut her off
Run my fingers over her intentional scrapes and bruises
I'm going to thank her for serving me well
Despite her age...and miles
And then I will park her …
And she will purr
Until it's time to ride again

The Arrival of the Poet

I came here with these talents
Blooms of visions of the wonder of God
And everywhere I was…I was free to explore
Until folks started closing doors
And marking parameters around my passion
Telling me what I should do with my talents
And implying what I could not do…
(Chatter in my brain just the same)
So I tucked my talents away
And claimed the ones someone else told me were worthy enough to prevail.

Passion, creativity, and vision don't belong on a validation scale.

So I reclaim and nourish what has always been mine
You never knew
But I came here with these talents
And that alone makes them more than enough.

A poet, like a woman, must remember
That the most important challenge
They will ever face
Is not the challenge to be heard,
But the struggle to find their voice
And use it.

Financial - In Dependence

For $50,000 a year
You put a smile on my face
Year after year
You have been allowed to find your way
Into this space
So near my scarred heart.
You're here
And you're not.
You never really unpacked…
At least with me.
But it's cool.
When you come this way now
I can't help but grin
Like a Queen on parade…
(I should add a wave)
I must BEHAVE.

You pay a price to see me smile like this
And so I do
On cue
A means to a life

Some things in life are priceless
But this smile
I know it costs me
Way more than it costs you.

Dead Weight

Why are sick people and dead people so heavy
Is it the absence of wellness, life, and the will to live
Or the absence of the spirit?

Spirit IS life...Spirit is light …
So life should be light

Why are you walking around so heavy?
Have you partnered with an elephant in a 3-legged race
Or are you dead?
Pulse check.

Eradicate the sickness
Infuse the spirit
A constant flow of energy
An ebb and flow
To flow
and sometimes to
JUST LET GO…

Stop micromanaging how your life will pan out
And just live it ...
Light

Live List

~~Conform~~
Transform
~~Wait for Love~~
BE Love
~~Self-Sacrificing Love~~
Self-Love
~~Luke-Warm~~
Heat Hot
~~Absorb Darkness~~
Project Light
~~Mute~~
Express
~~Internalize~~
Actualize
~~Escaping~~
Liberating….FREE
~~Doing~~
Being
~~Healed~~
Healing

Press (On!), Play (For the win!), Repeat!

Mile markers: Excerpts From the Vault.

Youthful exuberance:
If I can do all these things I can love you –
But what do I know about love?

Wisdom:
Wait a second
I gotta make sure I'm ME
Before I come to you.

Clarity:
Love isn't punishing
That, my dear, is Fear.

Radical Rebellion:
And the sight singes my eyes
And a siren in my soul screams
I'm positively pissed off
Do you know what I mean?

Self-Care:
I LOVE to laugh,
That is why I'm always cracking jokes,
Sure, my medication levels are a bit off
I prefer it that way
But mainly because I know a gut-wrenching laugh has healing power.
I don't use laughter
To hide my pain
But as an antidote
For its poison

Doubt:
Will I still want you to be my everything…
When you are ?

My Story…Too

I almost burned the house down
The day I put a candle where the light bulb should be
Replaced the shade
And set the lamp in the window
The carefully crafted, yet unconvincing illusion of a child
Who was poor…and ashamed
Of grown-folk business
Kept in the dark

Hovering so close to the coal stove
That I often burned my knees
Decades after the use of coal stoves was fashionable
It was all that was feasible
For the heat ran away with the light
And every day was night
With but a glimpse of dawn
I never noticed the film of soot that covered my arms
Until I was under the fluorescent lights at school
There were only the tears I cried to bathe my skin
I was dirty

And yet he found me
Invited me in to his place
And let me soak in water, heat, and light
I sprang to life each time I came
grateful (and afraid to lose it all again)
I bathed and rested
I was both safe and clean
But I felt dirty
As soon as he touched me
I never returned
But I would smell him
And feel him on my skin for years to come
Scrubbing and lathering
Trying to undo the soiling.

My Story…Too (cont.)

It was years before I got comfortable enough in my own skin
To set aside my mask
With friends I knew
I could trust with my heart
And then stand
without shame
In the gentle light of day
Embracing earth
Scooping up mud and minerals
Warmed by the sun
And applying it to all the surfaces that are raw and bare
Organically healing
The wounds that lie dormant, though not hidden

Delightfully dirty
Diving into a cool freshwater pool
To rise purified, refreshed, and restored.
It was a day
of healing
And preparation for…
The unknown
Strategically forgotten
Or still yet
to be written
and revealed.

Conversations with My Therapist #3:

I need help
Chewing my choices
And shedding my armored skin
I choose first
And I opt in or out
Assuming the worst will come
Unable to bear the reality
Dreading the possibility
Of not being chosen…(Or being unchosen)
It's like masticating razor blades
That relegate my tongue to a paste
I can neither swallow nor spit out

How old was I when I first felt unchosen?

Old enough for the imprint of pain and self-doubt
To ink a blue-print for my brain
On how to avoid that type of pain again
And yet ,
it still hurts.

Rotting flesh.

A confidence built
On avoidance at its strongest
A porcupine at its best
Keeping all a safe distance away
So they won't find the path
To the rawest spot in my heart

"The best defense is a good offense"
Both logical and paradoxical nonsense
As I stare in the face of my own problematic protection

It' s lonely behind my quills.

Conversations with My Therapist #3 (cont.)

They're embedded in my skin in clusters
Backwards-facing barbs
That slide in easily and come out fierce
If, by chance, I shed some
New quills grow to replace the lost ones
I can't seem to feel safe enough
to allow the tumescence of their erection

My senses are always heightened…waiting
Am I my own predator?

Shit!
I finally get it
I gotta get comfortable in the skin I'm in
Get close enough to my own heart
To uncover the festering part
That assumed because it was unchosen, it was unworthy.
Lean-in to the stench and the pain
As the pressure is released
And the putrid pustulence drains …
I'd rather be empty than carry this any further.

And finally perhaps I can see clear enough to live unbothered
Trusting the universe to select and deselect
What is to be

The ART of being chosen
Is simply
To choose me
To believe and know
no matter how it turns out
I am not just worthy…I'm entitled to this!

Mother to Son – A Langston Hills Reboot

There is life in the valley of a volcano
The sheer audacity of trees to rise
The grass to be so green
And flowers to bloom in the valley
Below the documented history (and real possibility) of destruction
Who are we, then, to wither and die.
The universe supplies nutrients unseen
We rise, so they must be there.

I am love, loved, loving, and lovable
You are love, loved, loving, and lovable.
Alive…even if not always understood.
Vibrant …even if walked upon
Flexible with the breeze.
Shed the old and create new
Branch out beyond the ash and toward the sun
Towards the heavens that give life
And feed the hearts of those who would dare
To appreciate and celebrate your beauty
All on its own.

Allow Me

If you know what it is that you desire
Just for a moment
Share it
If your mind will allow you
If you let me
I just might release myself
Free of inhibitions
Of expectations and restrictions
And come to you
Slide around you
Let you feel my presence
Elevate your temperature
Stimulate your senses
Mingle with your molecules
Synchronize with each synapse
Until you explode
Exhausted, yet pleased
As I curl up and rest
In a corner of your heart and mind
If you allow it.

Error

Such carefully selected snippets
You've collected
You out here slinging your facts
But I'm giving you my truth
Incorrect data points
Lead to
incorrect analysis
But I will help you with reentry
If you let me…
Will you open to this view
I am showing you
For it is me baring the uncertainty of a wounded heart and soul
But not of my affection and love
My heart doesn't lie, although at love it may fail
Will you erase those data points that have gone askew
And come to meet me… mask free
Or will I finally lose you
to your discomfort
with my self-discovery
and desire to heal

Bones

I really didn't expect him to fall flat on his face
I merely wanted him to lean and topple to the side
Slowly, like in the Matrix
(Since he was moving in slow motion anyway)
but without rising again
Just land with minimal impact
And I could tap him gently away
Delicately,
For him…and for me.
But NOOOOO!
He staggered backward
Like Fred Sanford
Clutching his chest, (as if he was alarmed)
Yelling to Elizabeth, or whoever would listen
That it was I who pushed him
But we both knew he wasn't planted.
I know inanimate objects can't move
But I swear he jumped
Into the crowd,
On purpose
Crowd-surfing, flailing
Creating a domino effect
With the sole purpose of destruction
And obliteration of all relevant connection.
There would be no scaffolding around him
For he would take the whole structure down
In a flash
Unstoppable, like dominoes on a run
Up and over, under, split, rejoining, and continuing on
Until all that was left was leveled bones
And I had no recourse but to forge my way
Through the path of destruction
That lay in my wake
A million micro-divorces
All because I chose to remove
One domino

Groupon

Groupon got to me
With its irresistible offer to join a wine-subscription service
A variety of bottles, interesting pours
Hand delivered to my door
It was such an amazing deal…
Then shit got real…

Holding a thin–rimmed goblet at the end of every day
Became synonymous with exhaling…
And oh how I need to exhale
Who has time to wait for lakes to form?
I simply fill the drum to the rim and let it slip down my throat with ease
Sipping it slowly
Sophisticated dipsomania - stewing in fermented bliss

I need to cancel this wine club
No more clubs for me
I'm already high on the wait list for
Club of the lonely , club of the hurting , club of those who can only find their voice …can only come alive with the help of a vat of something that "proofs" them…
The higher the proof the better
Argentinian Malbec, Italian Negroamaro, a French Beaujolais, A Toscana Rosa, a Napa Valley Brown Recluse or Chaos Theory
I traveled the world numb…
Seeing double
Yet none of what I needed to see
Puffy, yet empty
My liver acting as a sponge
and working harder than I was to make it right, every night,
To tolerate this life .

Thick accent thanked me for my year of insobriety.
Rejected my cancellation by gifting a 16 bottle case of the latest grapes.
Maybe next month I'll escape.

Fine Dining

The chefs of the finest 5 Diamond restaurants
delight my palate with dishes that require explanations
And lessons in history
I don't dare try to pronounce the names
Eager to let my taste buds unpack the mystery
I make mental note to google ingredients I have never heard of
But the truth is
My mind was blown before I turned 21
Nothing, nothing will ever top the feeling
Of going to Red Lobster for the first time
With the fella I was dating …and his fam
To celebrate his mom
It was a big deal
And I was dressed to kill
Blue and white sailor outfit
with a halter top and culottes
You don't understand
Wide brim red hat and red heels
And bright eyes
Taking it all in
I had arrived!
It wasn't the fanciest or the best
But what it was - was this
Me, gliding across concrete in the brightest sunlight
To sit in a warm space
Where there was hope and love
Where people treated each other as if they mattered
No cell phones scattered and only the ringing of laughter
And the welcome chatter of those who know your soul
And are charged with keeping it safe.
I was an outsider...looking in
And it was all I needed
A vision of how different life could be
It was the beginning of an awesome journey
A catalyst
And no matter how fabulous my detours –
That day was the first and one of the finest

Mr. Slurpee

I love the 90s ...Slurpees...and summertime.
In the back seat of your father's car
You were caressing me
And giving me a hickey that would be hard to hide
I was kicking myself, in my mind,
For wearing a body-suit -
The kind with two metal snaps in the seat
Already soaking with my juices
And those high-waisted leggings
That cradled the underside of the arch of my foot
The kind of clothes that would surely keep me from going too far
Too restricting, in a space too confined
To move and remove discreetly
But then, quick
In a blink of an eye your head was between my thighs
Cupping your mouth and blowing warm wet heat
Slowly, deliberately
Killing and resuscitating me
Each time you inhaled and exhaled
I tried to touch you ...to tease you
But you would not allow it
You parked yourself at the buffet
With a mouthful
And no intention of moving-
The fabric but a thin barrier
Soon I was dripping, begging , pleading, soaked
And saddened, certain that we would each be home alone
With huge wet spots and blue- balls
If I survived the nibbles on my clit
And your fingers trying to push fabric into a yoni waiting for you
You paused
Looked into my eyes
Placed one finger across my lips
And bowed again to worship

Mr. Slurpee (cont.)

I felt a breeze as you tented the fabric off my skin
Then ripped it with your teeth
Creating a hole
and a portal to my soul
Releasing the snaps
Parting the flaps
and then lapping
Your lips on my lips
Your finger just a few inches in
And the sounds of slurping and
Juicy-Wet goodness
unbelievably louder than my moans

I still hear the sounds of the multiple orgasms you gifted me
And I am instantly transported to ecstasy
When I summon you to my mind
To carry it over for those with less skill.
What you served was the ultimate brain -freeze
straight to my head
Sticky, wet, and the sweetest treat
I can never be finished with you
If only in my fantasy.

Seasonal Affective Disorder

How is it that I wandered North of the Mason-Dixon Line and stayed
I'm not supposed to be here
I abhor winter
Forced or selective hibernation
Scampering under the artificial light of counterfeit love
Half-heartedly reassured that I will be fine
That winter will end
Here it is the longest season
Without reason the mercury fails to rise
My engine stalls and stutters behind these walls of cold and gray
I have given away my power every season…until now
I am officially announcing the coming of Spring
No more waiting around for a scavenger to tell me when winter ends
How can I trust that he didn't see his shadow
(he can't even see me)
I will have nothing more to do with those predictions
And a sentence meant only to prolong my agony
I declare the coming of Spring
With these tears and this battle cry
Let its' rain come and wash away these chains
And Summer release my heart to the wind
Decidedly unbundled, unbound, and free
In a way that Winter will never be able to reign in again .

Inkin' My Thinkin'

It makes no sense to you
That I would circumvent my voice box
In favor of pushing a pen
But words get caught on my uvula
And it swells
Hot, inflamed, and influenced
By the parts of my brain
That rise to try to silence me
I choose this alternative path
The power of my pen proves too fast
For logical, rational, and restrictive interference

And you have ears that distort the speed of sound
Magnifying misunderstandings and
Amplifying fears of judgement, abandonment, and betrayal
Rooted in your bruised core

I'm inkin' my thinkin'
And it's flowing from my heart

Perhaps you should try hearing me
With another body part.

Trinity

She was. Then something triggered the split.

Along came Super-Girl,
with the youthful exuberance of a newly-minted superhero searching for validation
Simultaneously needing to believe and trying to prove capability and worth
By declaring herself the savior of her own story
and working to convince others that she could be the heroine of theirs
slightly naïve and mostly unaware
of the full range of her powers
and the presence of arch-enemies that would only be revealed with time .
Marginally evading spiritual death and sabotage
to emerge stronger
But with an ever-present nemesis of doubt
That was hard to ease, or please
But she would try
And she was I .

A crafty chameleon
Assimilating and shifting to avoid unrest
Transitioning into Wonder Woman
Vowing to do it all…at any cost
Quick to expend energy
Harnessing her thunder
as she rode the storm in invisible flight
Trying to save the world
Lasso life and draw it near
And stave off fear by doing …
Until she came undone

And then there was ME
Unfolding ………Unmolding
And flowing free

Trinity (cont.)

Peeling away the pretense
Surrendering the defense
Choosing to just BE
Divinely pruned
Authentic
Clinging to the essence of my soul
Setting boundaries
That honor my capacity
Without closing me in

Fractured identities enduring behind thinly-veiled partitions
Vaguely transitioning from one to the next
Across the passage of time
Never fully fading, never fully revealed
Yet I know they exist
Each waiting patiently
For me to understand them
And agree to join the pieces and parts
Shed the scars…and be whole

I am this Holy Trinity
Super-Girl, Wonder-Woman, and Me
An evolutionary riddle
Each providing clues and a compass
as I cruise to catch up to the woman the universe has destined me to be
Detoured, detained
But not deterred
from Her…
For she Is…I am…
Simply
ME.

Conversation with My Therapist #4:

Just for today
Let's not focus on how fucked up I am
I have these edibles and a strong 45 minutes
Of the one hour I pay you for
And the soothing sound of the fountain on your desk
And I am willing to share
And something tells me you could use the rest
So stoic and poised
I would have never imagined the noise that must sit in your brain
How do you have room for my chatter?
It doesn't matter, let me tell you this
She called-
I am on the list of your clients and friends
She feels impelled to tell
About your double life
You are helping us
While your own relationship
Is malignantly uncoupling
She raises questions of your sanity and your reliability
In dedication to annihilation
I know the sound of smothering anger
And truth peppered with pain and lies
She sounds weaponized
Reminds me of the pin-less grenade I have at home
Contained shrapnel waiting to erupt
And I finally get it …what you have tried for years to get me to see
Has it hit you yet - the high?
It must feel like diving into a refreshing pool
To leap into my fucked-up mind
And out of your own
Shit, I hope you have a therapist
Someone who stares at you while you face difficult choices
Someone you pay to help you figure it all out
I hope you still have trail-mix in your desk because I'm hungry now.
I hope you know that fountain is irritating as fuck.
I hope your years of training help you fix this quick and fast
Because next week I have more of my own shit to unpack

Inheritance

I am my father's child
I am my mother's daughter too
I see the humor in it now
Time wasted in youthful haste
To forge my own way
With indignation
Resisting being anything like them
Forming opinions on what I saw
(And thought I knew)
When they so carefully avoided showing all of who they were
Fragments I saw as weaknesses
Were but glimpses of the shrapnel that was their lives
A collage of highs and lows, hopes and fears,
high-steps and missteps, love and loss
The emotional (or emotionless) inheritance
that were the roots
which gave them source and sustenance
and at times left them wanting
needing
to heal
I missed the previews, the warnings, the cues
Before the struggle got real
And life happened enough to me
For me to finally realize
The secrets and the truths their silence held

I respect the man
And reverence the woman
Who could have fallen apart
But for an unforeseeable and unyielding glue
I am my father's child
I am my mother's daughter too

Lion Tame-Her…

He came hoping to make her purr
Playing all nice with Kitty-Kitty
Carefully petting, caressing
Gaging her response
Such a delicate kiss
But she was the type who preferred to roar
Arch her back and hiss
He wasn't ready.
He thought he could tease her with a single digit
She commanded a 5 finger salute
Searing pain
Blood
Her fluids
Clenching
Until she was lightheaded
Euphoric
Just South of unconsciousness
When she exploded
Releasing a waterfall down his wrist.
He was intrigued by what she allowed him to do to her…
Only she knew what she would do to him…
Soon
When he is ready.

Self-Parking

He waved me into a front-row space.
I thought it meant I was VIP.
I parked myself neatly inside the lines.
It was handicapping.
I ignored the signs that said
"No parking allowed"
And kept returning.
Although there was no validation given,
I still wanted it.
I never saw the ticket
But I felt the fines.
He was a hydrant I couldn't get close to .

Woman to Woman…Reboot!

We all hunger and thirst for something.

It was easy for them to think they were traveling alone
Each caught up in their own introspection
Two women met along the way
Down by a flowing rapid
Near the intersection of an exit plan
And a determination to stay

Same journey
Different direction

Trying to let the reflection of the weariness of her soul
Wash away in the ripples at the water's edge
She leaned over to gaze into the whitewater
Not yet wary enough of the turbulence that produced it
It was not an accidental dive
She wanted to sink below the surface
Submerging all of her despair
She had become an expert at gasping for air
She didn't register how much she could drink
Until the water called to her
Burbling over twigs and stones
Cascading around her doubts and fears
Of being alone
Cradling her in a cool, calm, riverbed
Where she could float and rest.
She frolicked there
Baptized into sin
And love
She rose, still wet
And reeling
In the folds of her blindness

Woman to Woman.. Reboot! (cont.)

She drank plenty
And lay drenched
Unable to quench a thirst
Born of pain
Even still, she found herself gulping handfuls
Simultaneously sending a waterfall down her throat
And a careless dribble from her chin.
The other,
Was as invisible as she thought she had become
Before her feet told her to run.
She wouldn't see her standing there
Until she heard her scream
"You thirsty bitch!"
She couldn't tell if the woman was calling her out
Or simply announcing herself,
(or both)
The sight of her called forth a memory
Of a mirror reflection
Empty ladle in her hand …
Looking parched
(Was she thirsty too?)

And what of the river running its unsteady course between them
Taunting them both with a supply
Hard to quantify, harder to contain

To drink or not to drink?

We all,
Even the river,
Hunger and thirst for something.

Show Off

Harmony found out she was being watched
Weeks ago…
When she was measuring the windows for blinds
And so when they came
she put them in the closet
unopened.
It was her ritual, you see
to shower
And stroll past in plain view
Open the window and allow the breeze to kiss and dry her skin
It made her wet again ...there.

She never met his stare
But simply paused
Oiling her body while singing softly
Knowing that he would crane his neck to see and hear as much as he could.

She knew HE would be watching
But it was HER gaze,
Unexpected and unfamiliar,
that she found herself drawn to…
It was nice
And it felt good, for once,
Not having to choose
Between being desired…
And being seen.

Rebirth

He jumpstarted her heart
Long before he hooked the electrodes to her nipples
Inciting a blur of pain, fear, and paralyzing passion.
He resuscitated her
And in gratitude she surrendered to him
As much as she possibly could.
The parts that were hers…were now his
They were forging an undeniable connection based on insatiable hunger
And a promise, a choice
To be vulnerable, naked, and unashamed
They wasted no moments trying to conceal their flaws
There would be no judgment here
Ever cautious and pensive
They welcomed their uncomfortable metamorphosis into risk-takers
Leaping into the abyss of the unknown.
Each bore the magnitude of their own complexities on their backs,
The weight of which only accelerated their descent.
What was there to lose?
Dead people know no debts
And they were each dying in their own respective cocoons.
Only the living can pay.
Even as they fed life one to the other
With spoonfuls of mercy and kindness
They knew it would cost them dearly
…but it would cost them more not to.
She would be his harbor
And he would be her haven
He would enter at her soul and free her
to take him in ways he couldn't even say he wanted to be taken
and in time
the numbness would end
with each erotic awakening
an alchemy of eros would unfold
until they were
born again.

Breaking and Entering

Aren't you cute
You think YOU'RE the cat in hot pursuit
When it is the magic between my thighs
That summons you here
I am perfectly clear on this
And I assure you that it is unnecessary to coat my heart with lies
For which other women plead
And bargain away their souls

Stop scrambling for a spare
It is useless here today
This door opens from the inside
And I hold the master key

You look stunned to say the least
No worries
Save your voice for filthy platitudes of praise
Come inside…
May the skin from these walls be bandages for your soul.

Ain't Nothing 2 Get Straight!

You will know my strength by the way that I forgive them

You will understand my grace by the way that I forgive myself

Bedroom Eyes…The Tale of 2 Wives

There's a thin, thin line
Between **PASSION** and **PAIN**
So hidden and discrete
That if you ignore that it exists
Then it almost ceases to be…
And so I think
As we lie, nude, on the bed
Stars twinkling in my head
Tremors casing the area
That once was my spine
Melting my soul
Cremating my mind
As your tongue
Then your teeth
Find my inner thigh
And nibble there
Until I start to sigh
And you can hear
Vibrations in my voice
Ignoring my soft pleas, Please
For you to stop
Devouring me mercilessly
Until all reservations drop
Multiple twinges of pleasure
Occasional Twitches of Pain
Noticed…but subliminal just the same
Insignificant in the burning heat of desire
As I call your name
Pain so sweet
It drowns in the broken sentences you whisper to me

Bedroom Eyes…The Tale of 2 Wives (Cont. 2)

Forget the 2 sensations firing to my brain
What else could this be but **PASSION**
No, not pain
As you pause and look into my eyes
Smile and ask me softly if I am pleased
Whisper that you love me
And call me by my name
Then explode inside me
With me
Like a tropical island rain.

Such a thin, thin line between **PASSION** and **PAIN**
So distinct, you know it's there
Your mind exits
Knowing your body won't be spared.

And then,
 without warning
He reaches under my blouse
Grapples at my breast
Dry, rough hands
Scraping my skin
Like #5 sandpaper on a polished oak desk
Sporadically twisting my nipples
Lowers his head – a warm tongue
Or so I think
Until he bites down
And impulses fire

Bedroom Eyes…The Tale of 2 Wives (Cont. 3)

Deeper and deeper his teeth sink into my flesh
And tears…
He darts up to my ear
Chews the lobe
Runs his tongue inside
It is wet
and cold
Before I can gather what we are doing
My skirt is pushed up
His pants undone
His breath
Hot…stale

His excitement
So rapid and quick
That it is far ahead of mine
And my eyes wander to the clock
To mark the passage of time
2 minutes from the start
My eyelids close as I try to feel…
Aware that I am dry
Like a desert
He tries to merge with me
Ripping resisting flesh apart
And I scream
NOOOO
I'm not ready yet…for this
PASSION, **PAIN**

Bedroom Eyes…The Tale of 2 Wives (Cont. 4)

He can't hear
Short jabbing thrusts
Squeak…the bed
And I cry out again
As the wall meets my head
He is there
Where he wants to be
Turned on by searing friction
He grunts a strand of profanities
And time…
Dutifully,
slowly,
inevitably
moisture comes
…Or blood

Just as my body surrenders and succumbs
His pace quickens , pauses, stops
He is done
I roll over
Touched
Yet painfully untouched
And Alone.

Peek-a-boo

Invisible or Blind
Is it possible to be both?
Can't bear to be seen as less than perfect,
It's no wonder that
no one can see you
falling apart
until
it is
inevitable.
Show up to yourself…
for yourself
Or face extinction

Sad News

When I heard the news, I felt such searing pain
I never asked how it happened
I was too afraid to hear
And since I hadn't heard the acceptable absurdity
Of a heart attack or a tragic accident,
I feared that the collapse meant
I had failed a friend
Me …and others
The keepers of ill-kept secrets.
We had seen the surface cracks
And knew where they lay
The chasms that ran
Flowing with life's lava that bubbled beneath the surface
Waiting to erupt through the fractures
And smother all signs of life
How can it be that sometimes not even joy
Can take the pain away?
The torment in a soul
Rarely shows through a carefully constructed mask
The one we all need to see
And believe in
Enough to fight our own fight.
Pain we see in others every day
Yet look away with uncomfortable haste…
Lest we look into a mirror at all our pieces
And realize how fragile we are.
I, too, have heard the chatter that shouldn't matter …but somehow does
Until I fight the night that makes the light to run and hide
Fight until I stand up bloody in the dawn.
Fully spent from beating back a boogie-man
That tries to seize my mind
And lock it down in a state of despair -

Sad News (Cont.)

I still can't bear to say the word depression.
Acute, chronic, devastating
I don't want to think about his final thoughts
On that final day,
That made him say
 ENOUGH!
And do too much.

Not sure if I feel guilty because I have known that kind of sadness
And been able to handle it
Or scared.
Because I realize
That but for my agility,
I too could surrender
To my fragility
And the next call you receive
Could bear sad news
About me.

Contract with My Therapist – I Agree to Live.

I knew I would bleed out either way
Knife in my back
Or stress weighing me down
An auto-digestion and erosion
That recognizes and respects no end except my own

So I took a suicide leap
That cursed and saved
Landing on a terrain
As rough as where I came from
Paused by a river,
running like me,
Confined and contained
With the illusion of being free
And then,
I kept moving
Letting go, this time
Of everything

Save self.

Third-eye focused inward
Healing
Instead of just watching my back
And trying to survive
It feels good to know that if I do it right
There is a chance that
I won't always have to run.

I won't take the knife to my wrist again
With any luck, I won't need to.

Straight, No Chaser

I had no more time to waste being fearful of you

I am perfectly capable of scaring (and scarring) myself

So I googled
"How to survive a narcissist"…
It worked.

Next I must google how to be less of one.

Altar Call
(For colored girls who have outstayed their welcome…..)

Revelations 1 on 1
You are all alone.

How long has it been since you danced
Unchoreographed
Allowed the true essence of your spirit
To move in human form?

You must first forgive yourself
For surrendering all motion
to a DJ spinning a tune
And forgetting to trust the beat of your own open heart.

When did you notice that the dance floor was empty
While you were spinning around and around
Or after you collapsed?
Is that why you sit dazed and confused?
Have you even noticed the silence in the air?

Why are you whispering in a club?
Because there is no music
And with it went your voice
To be written in the annals of history
Housed in a forgotten library of your mind.

Your glass is empty now.
There is no source here to quench your thirst.
I know it registers with you that
Everything has been cashed out
The bartender
Has tipped out.

Altar Call (Cont.)

You are paralyzed
And invisible.
The doors are locked
Closing you in,
Yet No alarms sound ?
You are no threat in this state -
Waiting for dawn
And a return.

Hoping to be discovered again
and treated as a welcome guest
and not an intruder?
Only those addicted,
Unconscious, or numb
Neglect to leave when the lights come on,
The music stops,
And the party ends…

Are you ready to go home to yourself?

Let's leave… before they all return
And lure you into investing into Club Yesterday
Waiting …
Honey,
Love is no longer being served
I can't walk for you…..but if you squeeze my hand
I will walk with you
At your own pace
Get up, Get up, Get up from wherever you are
And move…
Right now!

Sista

We were the very manifestation of synchronicity
She and I
Linked on the labyrinth of life
She spoke first
Eloquently sharing a spiritual download of
Infinite intelligence
And I thought
"THIS is how it looks
When a woman
owns her voice."
I was inspired by the soul-wealth in each intonation
A voice not newly-minted
(Like mine).

In silence, she watched
As I chronicled my pain
My words, a mentholated spray
Slipping from my tongue
And down a throat raw
From screams held in too long
Seeping into the hearts of those who recognized
Parts of my journey as parallel to their own.
She sat perfectly still.
Her face was wet with recognition
My tears and unfolding
A decongestant for her soul
My bruised heart an open stock- cock
For a free-flowing unfiltered voice
No longer hindered by valves of shame, unworthiness, and fear.
She emanated authenticity and peace
While an urgent knowing skittered beneath the surface of her skin.
I saw it there -
Both the encouragement to keep evolving
And the urgent warning
That even though you find your voice,
You can still be bound by things that conspire to enslave you.

Get Your Life

There's a thin, thin line
Between Promoting Self-Help and Helping yourSELF
And with the host of people
Dedicated to helping you "get your life"
It's hard to tell
Who is real…and who is memorex?
It gets easier
The second they lead you to believe
That absolutely ALL your thinking is wrong
They benefit from you not trusting your own decisions
Your gut intelligence and primal instinct
Your sacred wisdom under a spiritual guidance
And one on one consultation with God…
And the God in you
That they feel is a mere supposition
They can neither see …or understand
They summon you, (for a fee)
Promising that you got the right one
And they are correct...to a degree
You shouldn't do it alone
But Babyyyyyyyy!
You gots to be careful out here in these streets
Healing

Self-Care

Starting today

Take time to allow yourself to heal.

Resolve to love yourself
As if the person of your dreams
Were watching and taking intimate notes.

Shower yourself with incomparable love from head to toe.

Pamper the most fragile parts of your soul with loving kindness.

Let no poison enter into your body
Or permeate your brain
Safeguard the gateway to your mind
So evil, jealousy, envy, doubt , and fear
Can not invade, implant, or take root

Let all senses be heightened.
Allow yourself to be present and open to feel.
Open your eyes to see - with clarity
But without the need for harsh judgement
Train your ears to hear
Amplified by a discerning heart
Develop a hunger and a taste for yourself
your desires, your passions
Feed them and feast on them
Use your voice to speak your truths
Touch yourself intimately
Without shame or reservation
Mastering with perfection the ability both to please yourself
And to verbalize your needs.

Self-Care(Cont.)

Acknowledge your beauty and your strengths
Learn to give yourself more compliments than you reject

Walk in spiritual reverence of the presence of the Divine in you

Take deep, cleansing breaths and move with grace

No matter how hard life becomes
Keep moving!

So all will know without question
that you are God's child

Love yourself fiercely and unapologetically
So that whoever comes along
Will know
That opening your heart to love another
Is not from lack of love,
or a need to be fulfilled or made whole
But simply a gift
And amazing and beautiful gift that you give yourself.

Lessons

I love you.
I care about you.
That is real.
Not dependent on outcome
Not limited by distance.
Although expressed by, it is not dependent on physical touch.
My nature is erotic and sensual
But my freedom is not linked to orgasms
And I can not be owned by them.
They offer a release…but not THE release I ultimately seek.
Your friendship is important.
It carries influence because
you made room for my voice in your presence
As I stumbled to find my words
And the courage to confront some uncomfortable truths
About life.
Seeing has become mandatory
Not because I was choosing you or involved with you
You caught me with my mask down
And created a place where I felt safe to crumble
I move…even if I am stumbling
Not leaning on or using you as a crutch
Even when I feel I'm falling.
It's hurting , I'm injured
And I pause to bandage the wounds that I can only hope will heal.
I must learn to self-soothe, to stand, get knocked down, fall, get up again
Refusing to be done
I cry out
I am more than a ball of this pain
I don't have to just survive.

Lessons (Cont.)

I can move forward determined to thrive
To live fully, to love openly, to die empty
To explore eroticism and intimacy without it being secret or taboo
Exploring it as a woman who is treating her self
Not cheating herself...or someone else
Not shielded by a bubble
I will be still when I need to …by choice
Not frozen by fear, doubt, manipulation, or uncertainty.
I will move deliberately until my whole world is reflective
Of my unapologetic truth
With inner-flection… not regret

And I will learn from this journey

And a tiny little confining bubble
Will be reserved for all those things
That tell me to be afraid
All the self-doubt, the fear of loneliness and aloneness,
All the voices that make me second guess what my heart knows
All the judgement
Accusations of failure
Insinuations that I am not enough
Blatant or subliminal attacks
Unsolicited advice
And criticism meant to inflict pain rather than inspire growth.
I will remind myself that the bubble is not real
THIS Journey,
This road I am on
Is real, if yet unpaved…
And it is my heart's desire.

Ginger

I acknowledge that I hurt you
Believe me, it was unintentional
And so I offer you my sincere apologies
And pray, in time, I (and you) will forgive me

It seemed brutal at first
But I know, now, that it was
a sacrifice, a suicide, a homicide, and a gift-
Your Ghosting
Vanishing and Banishing
Dismissing and Diminishing me
Artfully dissecting so that in your heart and in your mind
I could simply cease to BE

Yanked my heart right out my chest (it still hangs there)
Like ripping off a bandage dried with blood
And with it, whatever eschar had formed
Exposing the most delicate nerves
Screaming in objection to the rawness of it all
And there was -
As you probably hoped there would be -
Fresh bleeding
Only healthy tissue bleeds.

But now I see
And I thank you
For doing what needed to be done for *our* healing
A prescription written in the universe
That I couldn't bear to swallow
So I just kept sweating it out
Hoping it would run its course
And I would somehow be made whole.
What felt like yo-yoing
Was not me toying with your heart and mind
But playing a tug-of-war with my own

Ginger (Cont.)

Wanting two things
That were impossible to do together
See you can be both sick and getting better
And that is its own version of hell…..
But you can't be sick and well
It's a contradiction
Like desiring to love you fully now
And simultaneously craving my own healing
Not just superficial changes
But deep-dive expeditions to the core
To unroof the surface and find the source of my pain
Incise and drain and then heal in stages
Stop the bloodletting with hemostasis
And with my heightened awareness
And an intact immune system
Defend with an inflammatory response
Focused on removing toxins, cancers, and debris
Until I am open
Clean, clear, and free to begin the real work
Remodeling, proliferating, growing
Then maturing and strengthening
Until I am healed.

To cut me out of your heart
You had to excise a part of your own
Our love (and the dreams of what we could be)
Became the sacrificial lamb
Harmed and destroyed for the common good
Grieving that loss is necessary
And I will do that too
And in fond ways I will always remember you

Your leaving made space for me.

I pray it has brought you sanity
I hope you know I love you
I hope you're somewhere healing…Gingerly.

*Musca Domestica (***The HouseFly***)*

The only people who take offense to you standing in your worthiness
And walking in strength and power
Are those who are afraid
That they can no longer predict or control you.
You start doing that
And they get to buzzing around you
Like Flies.
Think about it
They get louder and louder
Close enough to say something
That disrupts your spirit and your peace
And then…they dart away
As if they haven't done a thing.
They keep dotting in and out of view
They want you to notice
They want you so obsessed with looking for them
That you can not do anything else.
Like Flies.
They will boldly touch you, land on you, get in your space
And your body will respond to that touch.
It may be light, and delicate, and secretly welcome
But it will consume your spirit.
They will keep at it until they lose interest and give up …
Or until you get them.
You can waste your energy …and time
Trying to swat them out of the sky -
They like that.
They are teasing you, luring you in
Now you are playing their game

- A game of chance…not choice
- Skittishness…not skill
- Frantic…not faithful

You can do that
Or you can just wait
Be still…and wait.
Everything comes to the light
Rapidly they register hasty movement

*Musca Domestica (*The HouseFly*)* (Cont.)

Get still in knowing
For it is the slow hand that confuses the fly
It will come to you, if you be light
It has to …
If only out of curiosity about how you could possibly be so still
Watchful….waiting…pausing….knowing…believing.
You can raise your hand and strike with a certainty
That reflects your power
Or you can choose another way
Create a portal
Open a window or a door
You don't have to shoo it
(It won't go if you engage)
You simply have to let it go….
And then, close the portal.
That is it.
What you can not do,
What you must not do,
Is let it land on the things that nourish your soul
And then continue to ingest those things
when you know they are contaminated.
Don't let it fly into you…
In any way.
It is still a fly, by any other name-
Blow fly , sandfly, housefly, fishfly, dragonfly, mosquito…… fly
It has no place with you …and yours.
Protect your food
Protect your wounds
Protect your children
Protect yourself.
Don't lay out your spoils in unsafe territory
And whatever you do…
Don't dare believe that you are rotten enough
To have earned or deserved the attention of flies.
Claim your power and BE…Still
You are worthy of so much more.
Bzzz!

Friend Me

We've had some amazing times seasoned with patron or plant-based highs,
Elaborately crafted sips of life for thirsty souls,
Fast paced, erotic thrills for exotic tastes,
But the season for quickees, hang-overs, do-overs, once-overs, and makeovers is now done.... ....and I am sure some of you must leave.
I bid you farewell.
And to those who dare to stay...

Now bring to me the sober laughter that moves me to tears
A silliness that highlights the irony
Of all that would sooner break us then have us free
Let us laugh to remember that we can
And to forget, if only temporarily,
That which is designed for our destruction
Let's find the humor that yanks us back from the depths of despair
Enough to catch our breath
And journey on (unmedicated and un-numbed)
Past the do-overs
To where we won't need to rewind the clock to the time before we were unkind
Because you fucked up and didn't listen
Or I lacked the courage to use my voice...
Or both
Let's journey to a land where we can just speak our truths
And it not trigger your insecurities...or mine
Let's follow the yellow brick road to a foundation of friendship that is so stable and strong
That not even the most difficult conversations
Could cast doubt on the love, care, safety and concern
Simmering in our souls
A land where your need of me won't make me cease to breathe
And we can just sit with a genuine want, a hunger for one another
Neither smothered or alone
And let that be enough

Friend Me (Cont.)

Let's move to a field of possibilities where we quit hash-tagging relationship goals
And work with the reality of the connection we have…
and have the power to co-create
Before it's too late.
Just ahead , around the bend,
Let's enjoy an intimacy that … just …is
Not the kind that's undercover and too hidden
Or the type that has to be on display and broadcast for the world to see and so approve
But a soul-deep intimacy
The kind that seeps into showers wet with tears
Or sits in the dark spaces with keen ears for silent screams
That can only hint at the depths of pain
The kind of intimacy that saves again and again
And makes it safe to feel
That touches the seat of our souls and encourages us to heal
Cradles us with tender hands while we regain our roots
Yet holds us accountable for our own growth

Bring on intimacy scented with mutual love and affection
That treasures connection
And loves without the need
To makeover our ugly
But allows us to simply BE
Naked and unashamed
perfect and rare
simple and authentic
and most of all free.
Are YOU ready for real relationship?

The Procession

I was little when I was lifted high over a bank of snow
With strength powered by sheer love
I remember what it is like
To be cared for and kept safe.
Seasons bring forth change
and drifts of fluffy snow so bright
they blind like night with no end.
I think I am lost in a blizzard .
I have been living oblivious of self and time
Yet I am not alone
Someone walks with me
Silently marching to a cadence that feels …um…different.

I am above the ground
Slowly and carefully
Carried forth
As if I am precious cargo
And yet I feel entombed in darkness
The air is stale
But I am not sure how I can tell
My airway feels restricted
Obstructed
Smothered.
I try to shed the shroud that covers me
But it is tightly tucked
Why am I stuck?
I gather it's time to move myself
And so I will myself to rise
Nothing
Happens.
I cry out to them to stop,
let me down,
release me!

The Procession (Cont.)

I wait with no response
While the echoes of my anguish lie muted
By the shuffling of feet that are not mine…
Keeping time.

I am distracted, lulled again
By the feeling of being high
And a mysterious glide
I can neither understand nor explain

And then
It stops
And I begin to drop
Lower and lower
Down
And with a gentle thud I am on the ground
And for a few moments the world stands still in silence

I don't realize how far under I am
Until I hear the sound of the earth falling
And the wailing inside my head begins
Ignited by a moment of great clarity
Some of the people I thought I traveled with,
Were simply moving me
Grim-reapers disguised as companions
Announcing, pronouncing, and pushing me to an end
Where they could rise as self-selected pall-bearers
Committed to the rituals of burying the dead
Whose life they had come to pity, to envy, to take, or to mourn,
While they yet live.

Epitaph:
Be wary of who carries you.

Genealogy

I looked to find
And not to see
So I bear the responsibility
For what lie hidden in the periphery of my vision
My head coyly cocked and gazing
But not taking enough in
Through these prosthetic eyes I never knew I had
Until I prayed for the gift of discernment
(And surrendered to receive it)
Pray, surrender, work, exercise, receive , discern, move
Oddly enough - we came into focus
Although it required double vision
To see a panoramic view
of both sides of you …and me.
The image of who you were
When you wanted to be useful
A distorted projection of who you became
When you deemed me useless
The clarity halted my heart in ways that the withdrawal of love
(or my own self-betrayal) never could.
My very existence now was more than a result of my defiance
But evidence of divine protection from the disdain
of one who had always been practicing for my extermination
Just in case I ever tried him
Or tried to … be anything……on my own.
Isolation begets Fear
Fear begets Survival
Survival begets Defiance
Defiance begets War
War begets Surrender
Surrender begets Discernment
Discernment begets Shedding
Shedding begets Painful Solitude
Painful Solitude begets Peaceful Clarity
Peaceful Clarity begets Freedom
Freedom begets ME.

Like Maya

An invisible siren tucked beyond the trees
raises its shrill warning
Am I to duck and cover?
I am transfixed without refuge.
I find myself chasing storms that I should run from.

Night falls
But neglects to rise and depart with the coming of dawn
I am blindfolded by a wall of fog that rolls in
To swallow the sun in me
The imbalance creating a monsoon of
Pelting precipitation
That congeals in the spaces of my mind.
My thinking is unclear.

I imagine that I am Maya-in-the middle
Churning in an agony that pierces the soul
Like the moment she discovered that SHE was the caged bird
And just before she realized why she could still sing
From the depths of darkness and despair
I envision myself a Maya peering on the edge,
For a freedom that faith told her would soon come
Pushing her way through the black blizzard
To center herself
In a cloud-free eye
Where she could see and be seen
Defying the odds against
the flying debris of spiritual warfare
with an eerie calm
To rise…like a Phoenix…still.

Like Maya (Cont.)

I can only hope to be like her.
I will channel her spirit
And don Grace like a girdle
To hold my fragments together,
A coat of armor for what is yet to come

I release the grip on everything
Except the wonders of my mind
And surrender to move
In fearless free-float

Where-ever the journey takes me.

My release of control
Will disrupt the violent instability that has created this spiral.
Letting all that needs to dissipate
Do so.

I will myself to live.

These clouds will break before I do.

This storm will die

And I will rise…..Like Maya

Nipples and Wings

Nipples on men are curious things
Benign growths and trivial appendages
That are yet allowed to stay
What if they hold a purpose other than what we have been told
And have yet to discover
The uncertainty
Will make millionaires of opportunists who come
To sell boobs to lost men desiring to breastfeed babes -
As if the nipple and the breast
Are the foundation of what it means to nurture

……And what of wings on human beings
A bonus limb that is hard to appreciate
When you spend your life, (spin your life)
Always trying to land on your feet.
It brings to mind Icarus
And his benevolent Dad
Giving him a gift with attached strings
"You can have this beautiful thing
If you do as I say
And don't fly so near the sun"
Seems like a genius …but only after the fact
When the wings melted away
Careful genius… or just an educated guess
Some warnings are simply that
Fear disguised as wisdom
Maybe that was how it was for daddy dear
Or perhaps the unspoken truth
Equally malicious, if not sinister
Was an unacknowledged jealousy and envy
That the lightness of flight, and the absence of fear
Could send a seed soaring
Carried far away
From a planted parent
Like a breath of air on a dandelion head
Dispersing under the sun onto a field of possibilities
To sprout elsewhere…anew.

Nipples and Wings (Cont.)

Perhaps never to return.
That a son would find the courage and hunger others lost
(Or stocked away)
And dare to do, to see, to be …higher.

Generation after Generation
The cautionary tale never grows old
And beings flutter and flap their wings
Without ever taking flight
Head down, focusing on carefully planted feet
On a cobblestone road that never smooths out and never rises
And soon, when their quick pulsating rhythm
Seems ridiculous and tiresome
someone enters
With a logical explanation of why one should simply be free
of winged appendages
Clipping, with or without consent,
Or more grievous yet
Dropping seeds of doubt in souls
For self-inflicted trimming
And then sometimes, like vultures they come
Harvesting those very wings
Remodeling and molding them into Hope (Like man-boobs)
Selling them back to you
In self-help books and witty blogs
That promise to teach you how to soar……….

I wonder what Icarus saw as he soared high
Perhaps his brief moments in orbit
Face full to the sun
Riding the breeze
Were full of more wonder
And more beauty
than a lifetime of pecking around on the ground.

I hope I see you near the sun

Cinderella's Story….(As told by Cinderella)

I was an outlier in search of affirmation and validation
From sources alien to myself
It was an invitation, outfit, escort, and transport
To a Monster's Ball
I arrived to dance round and round
In jagged circles that spiraled
Into an abyss
Where two ends would try,
Yet never quite meet
For completion.

Living in the castle of unfair comparisons,
I desperately needed to believe
That I was worthy, beautiful, smart
Seeking validation in order to feel good
From those who didn't feel good…
Or perhaps felt threatened
And so could neither validate or support
Feet pointed and poised
To slip into fragile glass slippers
Of acknowledgement, recognition, and reward
A cacophony of oohs and aahs
Upon my arrival
Provided temporary relief from my reality
And a slippery slope that shoe-horns me
Jamming the most delicate parts of my being into corners
that make no room
The pressure and the sting a clarion cry of an ill-fitting existence
The throbbing begins
I limp forward
Dazed by the dichotomy of fashion and function
Much like the duality of love and hate
From those who in devious duplicity
Love to hate me and hold me down
And hate to love me when I rise

Cinderella's Story (Cont.)

Moisture wells within my eyes
And falls to wash away the carefully applied mask
 Behind which I hide
And I know the time has come for me to run
And let the costume fall away

You're wrong,
I never *lost* the glass slipper
I kicked it off,
Preferring to go bare
Because I could no longer tolerate the pretense and pain
Of the grace required for this masquerade

How did I get here?
Waiting for a clock to strike midnight,
Release me from this pumpkin,
And carry me
Home
 To
Myself.

You can keep your happily ever after
I am in pursuit of my Happily Now

Note to My Therapist:

I hope you never have to go to cancer support groups with 2 people during the same time period.

I hope you don't have to find one for yourself the same year.

Help me to deal with the reality
That there is no rhyme or reason
To who will live
And who will die…

Help me
With this grief
I am not ready to die
Why do I feel guilty for living

And yet lucky enough
To embrace with a sense of urgency
This gift of life.

Note to You

Something eats at us all.

What's your cancer?

What would you give to be
Cancer...Free?

Letter to My Cancer:

You cannot stay here.
You are a malignancy in multiples
Whose very existence
Renders me spineless
A crumbled heap that falls upon a floor
In shattered shards
No longer able to bear the weight of a world
That would not stop spinning for me.
In error, I assumed it was mine to carry.

I scream out, now, in agonizing defiance
No More!
And finally, I know more than I have ever known.
It is hard to believe that you were ever native to me .
You are an ungrateful and uninvited guest
You are not welcome here.

I refuse to be silent host to your hostility
When I am the one who feeds your very existence.
When did your symbiosis become sadistic…and why?
What might I have done (or failed to do)
To invite these unhealthy margins
Metastasizing and overtaking my boundaries -
Why did you think that I had none?

I will not shrink!
I will not recoil from your power to end me
Or a declaration and prediction of my inevitable demise.
I will not shrink like those who avert their fearful eyes
When they hear the news that I am saddled with the likes of you -
And you appear to be winning.
They run because they have no faith that I will be okay
If they can not "fix" it …..or me
Withdrawing for fear that I might hear the sigh that says surrender -
If I fight less, it will be quicker.

Letter to My Cancer: (Cont. 2)

I release them and count zero gravity to their fall away
For it is fear that makes them run bravely
From this cancer you share with me
As if it, and I, am contagious.

They promised to stand….yet off they go
Disappearing faster than the infusion of fire meant to incinerate
Every remnant of you from my life.
I voluntarily take in a medicinal poison
More toxic to every fiber of my being
Than you could ever hope to be alone.
I release with clarity and deliberate haste
Everything and Everyone that lays waste
To the trinity of my body, my mind, and my soul.

I reject you in willing acceptance
Of the aftermath of what I must do
To lose you -
There is nothing to lose as long as you have your grip on me.

This is supernatural, spiritual warfare
And I take no credit as my own
I have been divinely conditioned for this battle with you
And it is time
For me to scoop out the diseased parts of my marrow
In favor of a healthier me
One that stands
Cancer – Free.

Letter to My Cancer(Cont.3)

The grace of my fight will be a Testimony
A thousand beams of light landing softly in the hearts
Of those who know me
Who see my authenticity in ways you never could.

You will not be able to stop my ascension to a higher place
A place that you can never visit or call home.
I will savor it there.

I have no fear of my own demise
Though you may steal my breath,
You will not silence my song.

It is not your death rattle
But my own
That will lay heavy on the chest of all, far and near
A clarion call
Beckoning all
To find the courage to look
And see Cancer for what is.

I have found
The Key To Life….

I Will Love
I Will Laugh
I Will Live
And
I will Fight My Way
Cancer – Free!

For those who couldn't fight….but wanted to
For those who fought and won
Or fought and won a higher place
Your journey has not been in vain
I will honor you.
I will fight like I mean it
I will LIVE.
NOW.

SUPERNOVA

I twinkle really
And as such,
There are those who mistakenly believe
That I am an unsteady light source
I am aware of my scintillation.
The depth of my life spans a billion years or more
And I am living each one…showing up as me
And dodging the orbital debris that clutters the stratosphere
Shifting the atmosphere
And adjusting to celestial terrain
Again and again
To show up, rise, ascend , and thrive in the high place.
Am I sparkling then or a flickering flame on my way out?
It depends on who's watching, how close, and how open they are to unobstructed observation of me.
Some folk can only tolerate you when you flicker…
change your brightness or position, or adapt a transient inauthentic hue.
You're their favorite to stand next to
Because only when life dials you down can they show the magnitude of their grandiosity.
Have you noticed how they always pull you in as part of their constellation?
The gift of your essence has value.
There are those who will stand in clear view wishing upon the falling star that they assume you are.

SUPERNOVA(Cont. 2)

Don't pity me. I am not always at my finest in the darkest hour but I AM – everyday.
Come close if you dare
But be clear about your reason for being here
And truthful about your intention
No matter what you see now
Know this
Sooner or later
I am going to explode with intrinsic luminosity
That casts shadows on the sun
A brilliant burst of energy that uses every ounce of my power, my passion, and my purpose without regret
Even if it means that I am consumed.
I will cataclysmically uncap my core
and release the full essence of me
and if you are close for the right reasons you will revel in my radiance, vibrate with my victories, and bask in the heat of my glow,
All opportunistic gawkers.....will be fuel for my consumption.
I'm not just a pitiful twinkling star
I am a SUPERNOVA in waiting.

For my darling son and the daughters of my heart:

With this I have made you million-heirs
There are a host of things you will encounter in this world
And some you will inherit
You have ultimate power to define
Who you are and who you desire to be
Your journey is all yours....

Know that you never travel alone.

In this anthology, I share the thoughts of my heart and mind,
the lessons I have learned on my own journey,
and stories of those I have encountered along the way
So that you will know
the spoken and unspoken truths of generations.
As you discover your own.

Trust the God in you,
Trust your gut intelligence
Seek wise counsel and true friends
May you always have your voice
And find the courage to gracefully speak
Your authentic and unapologetic truth

Live Fully, Love Fiercely, Pray without ceasing
And let the journey unfold.

BONUS

Guess who else is "Inkin' His Thinkin" – My son!

Things I Don't Understand
By Winston Alexander Gillum

The world is a pretty big place
With so many different things
With so many different things that I don't understand
Why are clouds white
Looking like marshmallows in a cup of water
Why do birds sing the song of an orchestra
Why is grass damp in the morning
You feel it like droplets of rain against your leg
Why is Mom's cooking so good
Like Ambrosia when it enters your mouth
Why do we do wrong thing even when we know what we're doing
Why do we sin
Why do we take life from others
Why do we ignore what's happening around us
Why do we say there's a problem but don't fix it
Why does money equal power
Why is it so easy to get a gun
Why do we use social media to tear others down
Why is it that the news is chock-full of dreadful news
Why do we talk about people in a foul manner
Just because they aren't around
Why are we racist
Why do we steal
Why do we cheat
Why do we lie
Why are we addicted to stimulants
Why do we abduct children
Why do we abuse the ones closest to us
Why do we think it's entertaining to watch people fight
Why do we vandalize

Things I Don't Understand(cont.)

Why
Why
Why
I could go on for hours…
The world is a pretty big place
With so many different things
With so many different things that I don't understand
With so many different things that need to change

BONUS

The Ocean of Sapphires
By Winston Alexander Gillum

The soft silky sand between my toes was comforting
The sun's rays shining on the sea creating an ocean of sapphires
All of the kids playing suddenly stop
And for a second, time stops as well
The tree, a landmark of that day
The day we sent him
To the ocean of sapphires
The soft silky sand between my toes was comforting
But it didn't help to hold back the tears
The tears of grief
Though my pain was great
I was relieved his had ended
We each took a handful
Each step toward the water brought back memories
Of the past
And everything in the world was as it should be
The symptoms of acute grief were obvious
Crying, restlessness, and loss of appetite
It was late at night when I was informed
The sudden strike of pain seemed like a dream
No, a nightmare
One that left a hole where something important used to be
Something I loved
Filling the hole can take time
But filling the hole is what I must do
Because filling the hole with love is the only way I can survive the pain
The pain of loss
And the pain of sending someone
To the ocean of sapphires

About The Author

Phillis Cherie Mims-Gillum, MD, FACOG, CSC is a Women's Health Physician, Sexuality Counselor, and dabbler in all of the traditional roles women play.

Before labels, titles, credentials, and accolades...
Before someone told her that she couldn't make money as an artist and needed to get a real job...
Before all the naysayers and distractions...
There was simply...

Phillis Cherie.

Regarding her love for writing and her journey she says simply this:

"This life has taken me many places.
Peace, healing, and joy comes the moment I pick
up a pen and start inkin' my thinkin'
It's like I'm saying to myself...

'Honey, I'm Home'

Her son, *Winston Alexander*, is watching, learning, growing, and developing his own voice!
Enough Said!